HOMER, America's Traveling JACKALOPE

Written by Richard Lamb
Illustrated by Keri Green

Blue Balloon
BOOKS

Copyright © 2025 by Richard Lamb

Illustrations by artist Keri Green, represented by Beehive Illustration

All rights reserved. No part of this book may be reproduced in any form or by any electronic or mechanical means, including information storage and retrieval systems, without permission in writing from the copyright holder, except by reviewers, who may quote brief passages in a review.

ISBN: 979-8-3492-9332-0

Printed in the United States of America

This book was produced and published in partnership with Blue Balloon Books, an imprint of Ballast Books.

www.blueballoonbooks.com

I would like to dedicate this book to everyone across America who posed with Homer for a picture and sent that picture of them smiling to their family and friends.

My photo albums are a testament to open-minded people who have embraced jackalope humor and culture and who are now members of the Homer the jackalope fan club.

Once upon a time, there was a truck driver who drove a big truck all across America. He drove from Texas to California, from Washington to Chicago, from New York to Florida, and to many more states. He brought Homer the jackalope along on his adventures, and they traveled together for thousands and thousands of miles.

Many times, Homer was brought into a motel where the owner had never seen such a mysterious furry rabbit with horns. Sometimes, Homer was petted by motel owners from India, which made them smile.

Often, they would have their pictures taken with Homer so they could show their family and friends.

Sometimes, the driver would see a fireman by his fire truck and ask if he would like to have his picture taken with Homer. After all, he was a special jackalope who had traveled all across America! Many smiling firemen did snap a photo when they held Homer by their big red trucks in cities like Dallas, Texas, and Trinidad, Colorado.

Smiling policemen in North Carolina and New Mexico had their pictures taken with Homer as well.

Even horseback riders have had their pictures taken with Homer in a national forest by Cloudcroft, New Mexico.

Homer was in a Fourth of July parade in Cloudcroft, New Mexico.

He was also in a Port Aransas, Texas, parade where people put colorful beads on his horns.

Campers have had their pictures taken with Homer in many locations in New Mexico, including in Sugarite Canyon State Park by the Colorado border. Visitors from Korea, Germany, and Iran have also enjoyed capturing a photo with the friendly jackalope so they could send them back to their friends and families in their home countries.

Homer survived Hurricane Harvey which slammed into the Texas coast in 2017 and came from the Gulf of Mexico with very destructive winds and extreme flooding.

Homer rode on the Grand Canyon Railway in Arizona. He was also on the Great Smoky Mountains Railroad in North Carolina.

If you saw pictures of Santa Claus holding Homer, would you want a photo with Homer too? Santa saw Homer in Rockport, Galveston, and Austin, Texas. Santa said that Homer sure traveled a lot—and let loose a hearty laugh!

A pilot standing by his plane was happy to see Homer in Texas.

Have you ever seen a hot air balloon? It's a big balloon that floats in the sky and carries people in a basket. Homer rode in a hot air balloon with many colorful balloons around him in Raton, New Mexico.

Homer met two traveling bicycle riders who were riding from California to Florida in Pancho Villa State Park by the Mexican border.

Have you been to Redwood National Park in Northern California? That's where you can find the tallest trees in North America.

Homer has also been to Plymouth Rock in Massachusetts. How far is Plymouth, Massachusetts, from Rockport, Texas?

Grinning Saint Patrick's Day teachers dressed in green enjoyed their photo op with Homer. If you saw pictures of smiling people such as campers, horseback riders, firemen, policemen, and people with jackalope tattoos on their arms and legs, would you want your picture taken with Homer? Everyone smiles while holding Homer!

Homer was at the 50th Annual Chili Cook-Off in Terlingua, Texas, which is near Big Bend National Park in West Texas. How far is Big Bend National Park from Rockport?

Homer has been to Dubois, Wyoming, where there are many jackalopes. Some are so big you can sit on them.

Homer has been to many birthday parties, including one for a sixty-five-year-old man in New York and a ninety-year-old grandmother in Dallas, Texas.

Homer had his picture taken with two female coffee drinkers from Amsterdam who were tourists in a ghost town in West Texas. Imagine the look on their faces when they saw a jackalope!

Homer had his picture taken at a vineyard in Paris, Arkansas, where they grow grapes. Have you ever been to a vineyard?

Homer had his picture taken with some visitors from China at Niagara Falls in New York. Many people got photos with him there. How far is Niagara Falls from Rockport, Texas? It is by Canada, so it is very far.

Homer was on the Appalachian Trail near Franklin, North Carolina. He had his picture taken with many hikers carrying backpacks. How far is Franklin, North Carolina, from Rockport?

Homer has been to Sturgis, South Dakota, where many thousands of motorcycle riders go every summer in August. How far is South Dakota from Texas? Homer is lucky to have been there twice.

Imagine you are a fast-food worker at a drive-through window and a driver shows you Homer when he places his order. Many fast-food workers smile and laugh. They are happy to have a customer with a good sense of humor.

Homer visited Odessa, Texas, which has a jackalope mascot for their hockey team.

A visit to the Port Isabel famous lighthouse was on his bucket list.

Homer visited a famous ranch in Kingsville, Texas, where he saw Texas longhorns.

The world famous whooping cranes come to the Aransas Wildlife Refuge by Rockport, Texas, and bird lovers flock to this area from all over the world.

As you can see, Homer has been to many places in America over twenty years. When strangers see pictures of a traveling jackalope named Homer, they are happy to have their pictures taken with him as well.

Homer is a magical, traveling friend who makes people smile all across America! Wouldn't you smile, too, if you met Homer, America's traveling jackalope?

Richard Lamb has lived quite a storied life, having been an educator, sailing instructor, and truck driver. He even has a background as an author, having published *A Ghost in Maritime America* in 2023.

Richard enjoys using Homer to put a smile on people's faces in campgrounds, motels, and cafés as well as at events as he travels. He is eager to more broadly share the joy that Homer brings with the publication of *Homer, America's Traveling Jackalope*!

Homer may be America's traveling jackalope, but it wasn't just friendly American faces that he charmed with his quiet charisma. Homer drew curiosity from visitors from across the world.

There was the thoughtful English teacher, all the way from the Netherlands, who paused for a snapshot with the legendary creature.

Two warm-hearted women from Amsterdam, sharing coffee in the Texas town of Terlingua, couldn't resist capturing a memory with Homer.

Even a stylish young woman from China, sporting a New York t-shirt, made a special stop to meet the beloved jackalope.

Lost but in good spirits, a hiking couple from Juarez took a delightful detour by posing with Homer, taking home a truly unique souvenir of their unexpected forest adventure.

The sweet aroma of faraway pastries seemed to follow the Cambodian baker who eagerly awaited her turn for a picture.

And the young woman from Switzerland, embracing the spirit of the West with her cowboy hat, beamed as she stood beside Homer.

The welcoming Indian motel owners, one with a vibrant red bindi, shared smiles and a moment with the well-traveled jackalope.

Even the adventurous hot air balloon owner from Kenya, whose voice carried a British accent, was captivated by Homer's gentle presence.

From Europe to Asia, from North and South America to Africa, these international travelers, each with their own stories and backgrounds, were united by a shared curiosity and drawn in by the undeniable appeal of this unique American jackalope. Homer, in his unassuming way, became a truly global phenomenon, one smile and one snapshot at a time.

www.ingramcontent.com/pod-product-compliance
Lightning Source LLC
LaVergne TN
LVHW071701060526
838201LV00038B/401